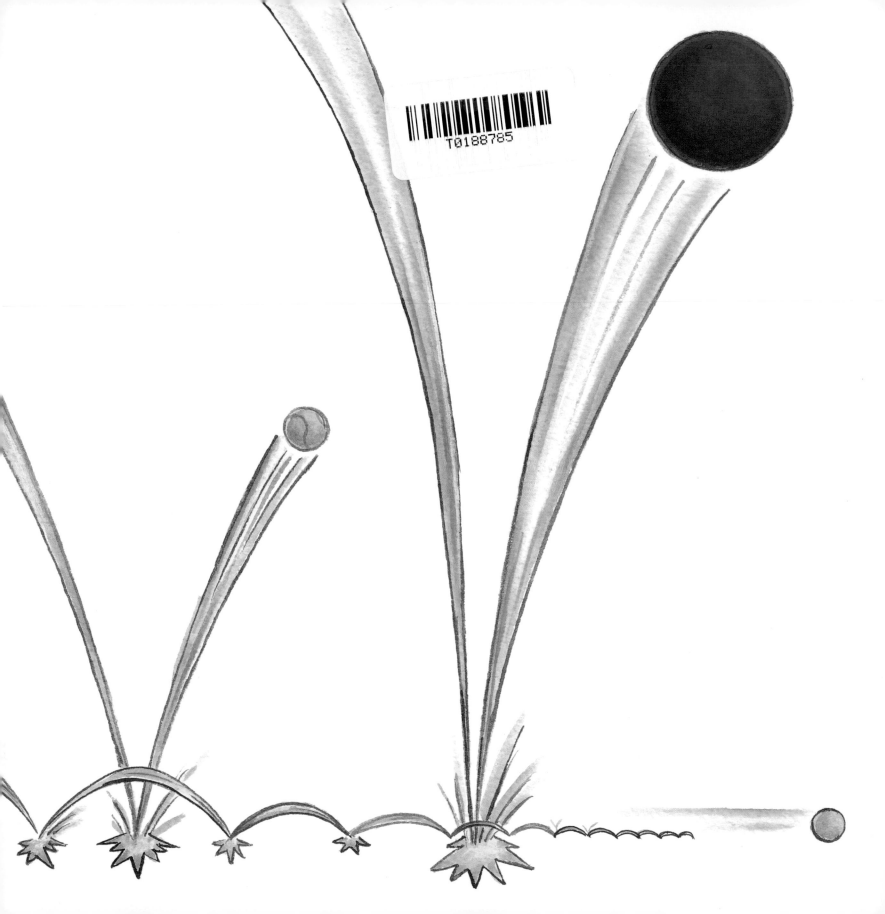

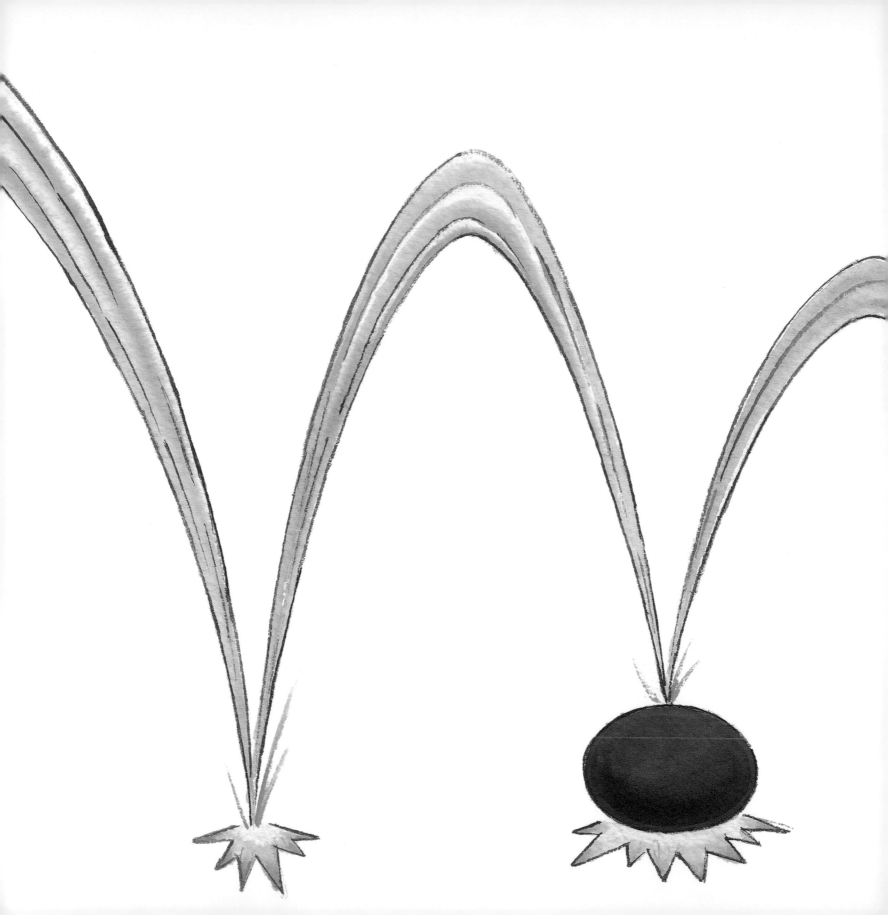

BOUNCE!

A Scientific History of Rubber

Sarah Albee   *Illustrated by* Eileen Ryan Ewen

Charlesbridge

It can BOUNCE, BOUNCE, **BOUNCE!**

It can **stre-e-e-e-etch**.

It can be molded and shaped.

It can r o o o o o o l l.

It can even float.

It's RUBBER!

Who discovered it?

Where does it come from?

How is it made?

Rubber has been around for thousands of years. Natural rubber comes from plants.

In parts of Mexico and Central America, people living close to the rainforest collected a milky-looking liquid from certain types of trees.

The liquid is called latex.

They mixed it with the juice of a special vine, then boiled the liquid slowly over a smoky fire until it became . . . rubbery.

They made many things with it, including bouncy rubber balls for playing games.

Back in Europe, balls had never been very bouncy.

Leather ball stuffed with feathers.

ANCIENT ROME

THE MIDDLE AGES

Blown up animal bladder stuffed with dried peas.

Not bouncy.

THE RENAISSANCE

About five hundred years ago, some Spaniards splashed ashore in a land that had long been home to many Indigenous people.

They called the place the "New World," but it was "new" only to the Europeans.

While their main goal was to find gold and silver, the Spanish noticed people playing a curious game.

The bounciness of the ball astounded the Europeans.

When those Spanish invaders sailed back to Spain, their ships were loaded with stolen gold, silver, and also—some of those mysteriously bouncy balls.

A later ship brought over some players, too. The Europeans were fascinated by their ball game. At the time neither the Spanish nor the English language had a word that meant *bounce*.

What makes rubber bounce?

Rubber can be squished, and stre-e-e-etched, and can then spring back to its original shape.

During a bounce a rubber ball squishes ever-so-slightly against the ground. When it hits the ground, the ground pushes it back up.

But because rubber molecules have a special springy quality, the ball quickly unsquishes to its original shape and boings back up again.

As rubber from the "New World" bounced from one European country to another, people found many uses for it.

Someone discovered that a glob of the stuff could rub out mistakes. (Before rubber, most people's go-to eraser had been a morsel of moist bread.)

Erasers are still called rubbers in England.

In the American colonies, where city streets could be
unpaved and muddy, rubber boots became a hit.

In England a scientist named Michael Faraday
cut out two rubber circles and stuck them
together to invent the first rubber balloons.

But he didn't create them for
birthday parties.

Faraday used the rubber balloons
in the laboratory to perform
experiments with gases.

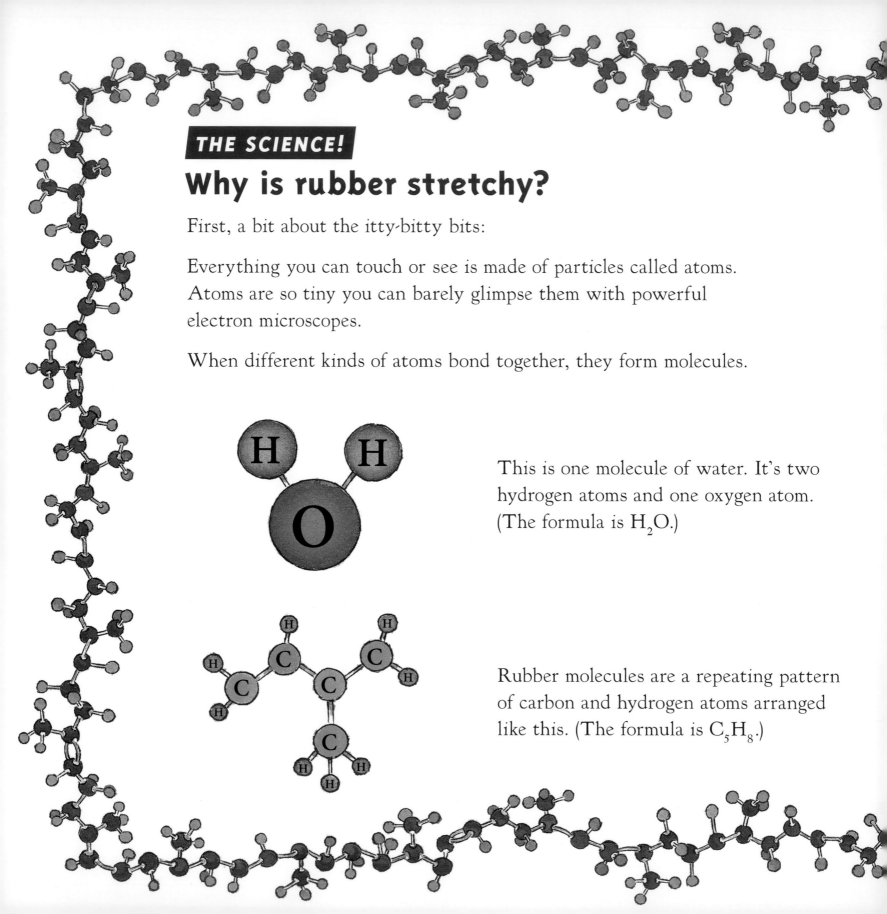

Why is rubber stretchy?

First, a bit about the itty-bitty bits:

Everything you can touch or see is made of particles called atoms. Atoms are so tiny you can barely glimpse them with powerful electron microscopes.

When different kinds of atoms bond together, they form molecules.

This is one molecule of water. It's two hydrogen atoms and one oxygen atom. (The formula is H_2O.)

Rubber molecules are a repeating pattern of carbon and hydrogen atoms arranged like this. (The formula is C_5H_8.)

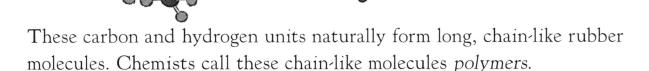

These carbon and hydrogen units naturally form long, chain-like rubber molecules. Chemists call these chain-like molecules *polymers.*

Rubber polymers are *really* long and *very* stretchy. One rubber polymer can contain thousands and thousands of identical, repeating C_5H_8 units, all tangled up like cooked spaghetti.

$$H_3C \quad\quad H \quad\quad\quad\quad\quad CH_2 \quad\quad H_3C \quad\quad H$$
$$C=C \quad\quad CH_2 \quad\quad C=C$$
$$H_2C \quad\quad CH_2 \quad\quad CH_2 \quad\quad CH_2$$
$$H_3C \quad\quad H$$

natural rubber

When you stretch rubber, the tangled polymers straighten out and can extend to several times their normal length.

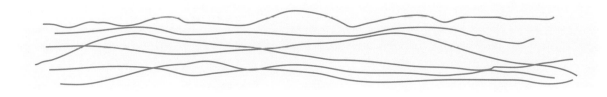

When you let go, the polymers snap back into their tangled-spaghetti state.

Materials that stretch and snap back like this are described as being elastic.

A man named Charles Macintosh put a layer of rubber between two layers of thin cloth. The first raincoats? For people in Europe and the United States, yes. Raincoats became all the rage.

Meanwhile, people in the rainforest had been making waterproof rubber cloaks for thousands of years.

But soon a sticky situation emerged. People discovered that their rubber clothing got gooey and stinky in hot weather. And got hard and brittle in the cold.

Hot temperatures turned rubber to goop.

Cold temperatures made rubber hard and crackly.

Why does rubber melt in the heat and get brittle in the cold?

A rubber polymer.

In warm temperatures, these connections get weaker, and the rubber turns to goop.

In cold temperatures, these connections become more rigid, and the rubber turns hard and brittle.

The craze for rubber products abruptly ended.
Factories closed. Everyone agreed: rubber was useless.
Or was it?

In America Charles Goodyear set out to solve the problem of
sticky, stinky rubber. But Goodyear was not a trained chemist.
He was a tinkerer. Also, he was constantly short on money.

For years Goodyear tinkered. His family often went hungry.
Neighbors complained about the smells. But he kept experimenting.

One day Goodyear tried mixing sulfur into rubber.
A breakthrough! The mixture seemed less sticky.
He mailed samples of his sulfury rubber to other
laboratories, hoping to interest people in sending
money for his research.

Goodyear continued to tinker. And then one day
he stumbled on the solution: *heating* the sulfur-rubber
mixture caused rubber to hold its shape!

Meanwhile, Goodyear had no idea things were also heating up over in England. Two of his sulfury-rubber samples arrived in the laboratory of Thomas Hancock. An excellent chemist, Hancock understood that Goodyear's mixture was a game-changer. All it needed, Hancock realized, was heat. Both men solved the puzzle: *heating* Goodyear's mixture created a strong, stable rubber. Hancock called the process vulcanization, after Vulcan, the Roman god of fire.

How can rubber be molded and shaped?

When you combine sulfur with rubber and then add heat and pressure, the long polymers connect to one another in a process called *cross-linking*. The sulfur atoms link with the carbon atoms in more than one molecule, like rungs on a ladder.

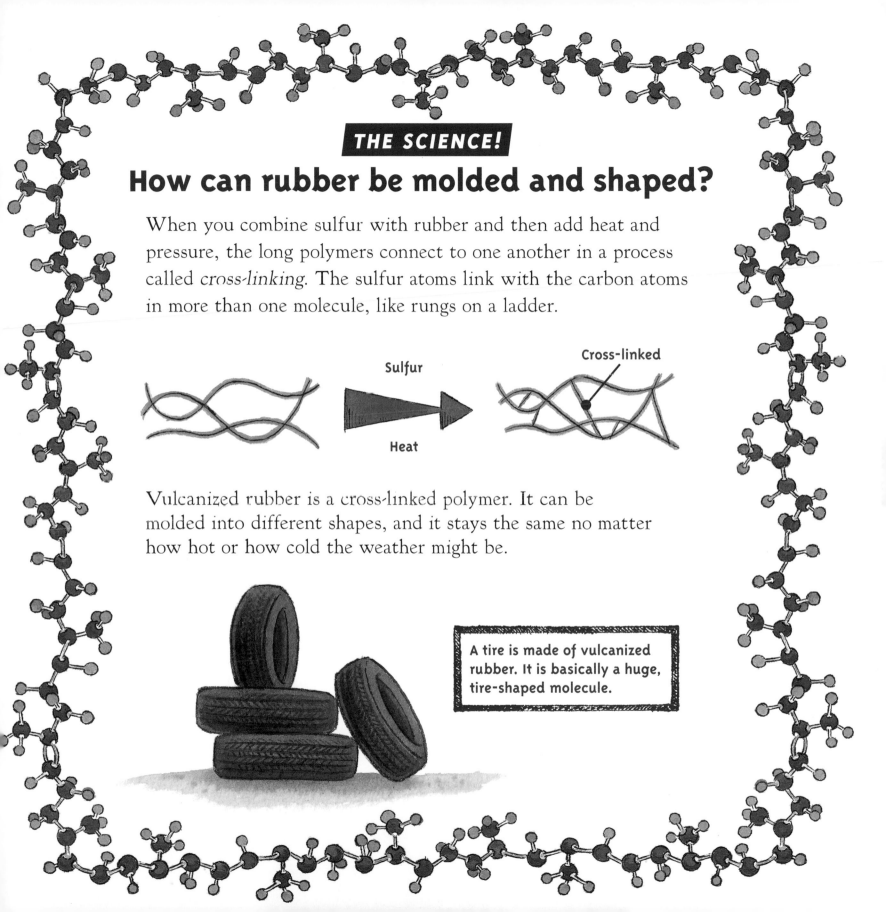

Sulfur

Heat

Cross-linked

Vulcanized rubber is a cross-linked polymer. It can be molded into different shapes, and it stays the same no matter how hot or how cold the weather might be.

A tire is made of vulcanized rubber. It is basically a huge, tire-shaped molecule.

Both men filed patents at nearly the same time— Hancock in England, Goodyear in the United States. Hancock became wealthy. Goodyear never did. But Goodyear discovered the secret first.

This remarkable vulcanized rubber didn't melt in the heat or crack in the cold. The result? New and exciting inventions exploded onto the scene.

Special rubber-soled shoes
became wildly popular.
People called them sneakers
and wore them to play sports.
And now they could play
games with balls that bounced!

And then along came
a new craze. . . .

Bicycle riding!

The new bikes had rubber tires filled with air.

Older bikes with
wooden wheels
were called
bone-shakers.

And then came **automobiles!**

When cars became cheaper, the world wanted wheels!

THE SCIENCE!

What makes rubber roll?

Flexible rubber molecules can squeeze into the uneven surfaces of roads and sidewalks and help tires grip the surface.

As the demand for rubber bounded ever higher, scientists finally figured out how to make synthetic rubber in the laboratory. They used petroleum products instead of natural rubber from plants. Soon enough, scuba diving suits, bubble gum, and many types of inflatable boats were being made with synthetic rubber.

THE SCIENCE!

Why can rubber float?

In its solid form—such as a rubber eraser—rubber can be denser than water and will sink.

But a rubber beach ball filled with air is much less dense than water, so it will float.

Rubber is really rather remarkable. After all,

it can BOUNCE, BOUNCE, BOUNCE!

It can **stre-e-**  **e-e-etch**.

It can be molded into shapes.

It can *roooooooll*.

It can even float.

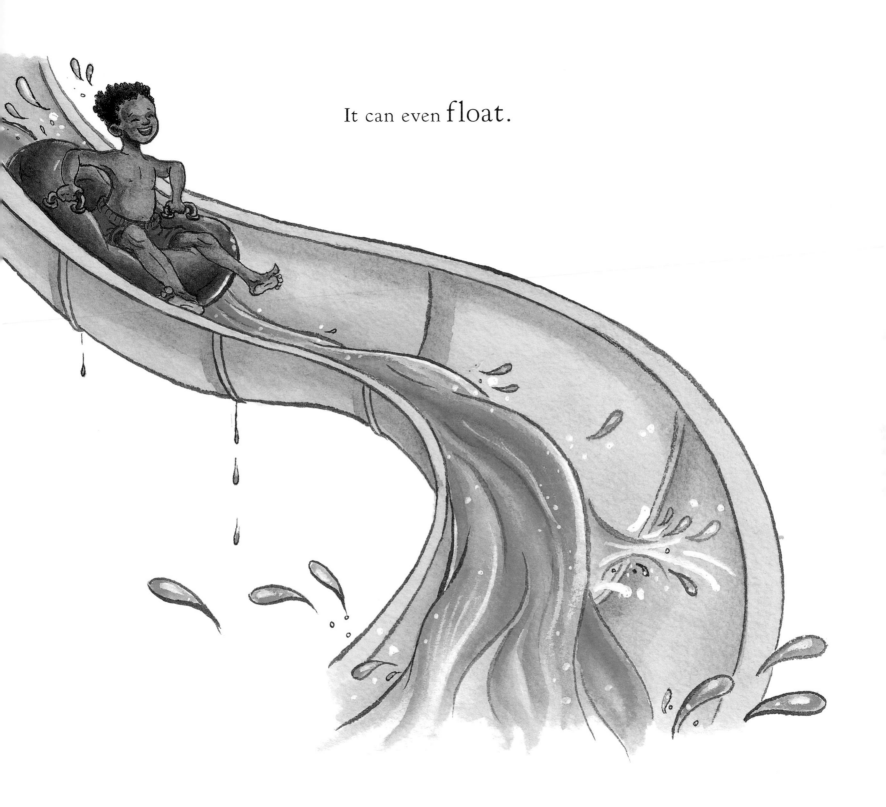

What would we do without rubber?

A Note about Names

Today, most people who are descendants of the original inhabitants of the Caribbean islands, Mexico, Central America, and South America prefer to be known by the names of their individual nations. But sometimes those names can be complicated. The name for the Olmec civilization comes from the Nahuatl (Aztec) language and means rubber people. We don't know for certain what the Olmec called themselves. The Aztec empire is now commonly referred to as the Triple Alliance. In this book the broader term Indigenous has been used for people who inhabited a place prior to the arrival of foreigners and is generally accepted as neutral and respectful.

Author's Note:
Some Deeply Disturbing Details about Rubber

In this book I have focused on the scientific history of rubber. But it's important to recognize that the discovery and production of this remarkable product has a troubling and often-violent backstory.

Our modern world could not function without rubber. But since its first introduction, the demand for rubber by colonial rulers and rubber producers has caused ongoing misery for millions of Indigenous people. Latex-harvesting workers have been mistreated, enslaved, overworked, and all too often killed. These atrocities have happened in Mesoamerica, South America, Central Africa, Southeast Asia, and other areas where natural rubber grows.

Nowadays most natural rubber comes from Southeast Asia and Central Africa. And even today, many people who harvest and process natural rubber work long hours, receive low pay, and lead very hard lives.

The demand for rubber has also created huge environmental problems:

- Vulcanized rubber is difficult to recycle. This is a big problem when you consider that world-wide, a billion rubber tires are thrown away every year.

- Although natural latex is biodegradable, most rubber balloons are made of chemically treated latex and may last for months. Deflated balloons can be dangerous to birds and sea animals. If an animal tries to swallow a balloon, it can lodge in the animal's digestive tract.

- Producing synthetic rubber requires a great deal of energy and water, and can pollute the environment. And for many products, including automobile and airplane tires, synthetic rubber is considered inferior to natural rubber.

Time Line

3,500 years ago:

People from ancient civilizations who live in what is now called Central America harvest rubber from different species of trees. They make many products with it, including medicines,  clothing, footwear, adhesives (sticky things), and bouncy balls.

1493:

On his second voyage, Christopher Columbus and his men see Indigenous people playing with rubber balls in an area now called Haiti.

1519:

Hernán Cortés invades what will later be called Mexico and conquers the Aztec civilization (also known as the Triple Alliance) in the name of Spain.

1528:

Cortés brings some Indigenous athletes back to Spain, where they play exhibitions of their ball games. Europeans are astounded by the bounciness of the rubber balls.

1700s:

People of the Amazon (in parts of South America) begin tapping *Hevea brasiliensis* rubber trees. This is the type of rubber that will become popular in Europe and America.

1770:

English scientist Joseph Priestley notes that rubber works great as an eraser (or rubber).

1820:

Thomas Hancock opens a rubber factory in London. Rubber footwear from South America is sold in the United States.

1823:

Charles Macintosh starts producing waterproof fabric and raincoats. He markets the raincoats as Mackintoshes (with an added k in the name).

1824:

Michael Faraday creates the first rubber balloons, for laboratory experiments.

1839:

Charles Goodyear creates the first vulcanized rubber after years and years of trying.

1842–3:

After examining some of Goodyear's rubber samples, Thomas Hancock realizes that the combination of sulfur, rubber, and heat can stabilize rubber.

1843:

Goodyear files a patent for vulcanized rubber in the United States. Hancock files a patent for the discovery in England.

1845:

The first rubber bands are patented by Stephen Perry and produced by Messrs Perry & Company in England.

1861:

For the first time, rubber products play a major role in war. Union armies in the American Civil War wear rubber ponchos, carry rubber flasks, and pitch rubber tents.

1863:

Rules are drawn up for the modern version of soccer (known as football in many countries). The game becomes wildly popular, thanks to the invention of balls made from vulcanized rubber.

1876:

Henry Wickham collects thousands of rubber seeds in Brazil and ships them to England. Eventually the seeds will be sent to British colonies in Asia, where rubber plantations will become established.

1885:

The first motor car is produced in Germany.

1887:

Although air-filled rubber tires were first patented in 1845, Scottish inventor John Boyd Dunlop generally gets the credit for the invention after he replaces the solid rubber tires on his son's tricycle with air-filled rubber tires.

1889:

The Dunlop Rubber Company begins producing air-filled rubber tires for bicycles, and later, for motor cars.

1890s:

The arrival of ever-more-affordable gasoline-powered automobiles leads to a growing demand for rubber tires.

1891:

James Naismith invents the game of basketball. Early games are played with soccer balls.

1898:

The Goodyear Tire & Rubber Company is established in Akron, Ohio. Although named after Charles Goodyear, the company has no connection to him.

1905:

More and more rubber is exported from British colonies in Malaysia and Sri Lanka. British investors make a fortune.

1909:

Scientists at the Bayer laboratory in Germany successfully create a form of synthetic rubber.

1930:

A team at the DuPont company, led by Wallace Carothers, develops a synthetic rubber that will eventually be called neoprene. (In 1935, Carothers will also invent nylon.)

1947:

Inventor Peter Ganine patents the rubber duckie float toy.

Today:

Approximately half of all rubber produced is natural rubber.

Selected Bibliography

Cross, Rod. "Impact Behavior of Hollow Balls." *American Journal of Physics* 82, no. 3 (2014): 189–95.

Gough, J. A. "A Description of a Property of Caoutchouc, or Indian Rubber; with Some Reflections on the Cause of the Elasticity of This Substance." *Memoirs of the Literary and Philosophical Society of Manchester* 1 (1805): 288–95.

Gray, Theodore W. *Molecules: The Elements and the Architecture of Everything.* New York: Black Dog & Leventhal, 2018.

Hochschild, Adam. *King Leopold's Ghost: A Story of Greed, Terror, and Heroism in Colonial Africa.* New York: HarperCollins, 2020.

Hosler, Dorothy, Sandra L. Burkett, and Michael J. Tarkanian. "Prehistoric Polymers: Rubber Processing in Ancient Mesoamerica." *Science* 284, no. 5422 (1999): 1988–91.

Jackson, Joe. *The Thief at the End of the World: Rubber, Power, and the Seeds of Empire.* New York: Penguin Books, 2009.

Keoke, Emory Dean, and Kay Marie Porterfield. *American Indian Contributions to the World: 15,000 Years of Inventions and Innovations.* New York: Checkmark Books, 2003.

Mann, Charles C. *1493: Uncovering the New World Colombus Created.* New York: Knopf, 2011.

Michalovic, Mark. "The Story of Rubber," Polymer Science Learning Center. https://pslc.ws.

Quarterly Journal of Science, Literature and the Arts, v. 17, London: John Murray, 1824.

Slack, Charles. *Noble Obsession: Charles Goodyear, Thomas Hancock, and the Race to Unlock the Greatest Industrial Secret of the Nineteenth Century.* New York: Hyperion, 2002.

Strutt, Joseph. *The Sports and Pastimes of the People of England: From the Earliest Period.* London: William Tegg, 1845.

Tarkanian, Michael J., and Dorothy Hosler. "America's First Polymer Scientists: Rubber Processing, Use and Transport in Mesoamerica." *Latin American Antiquity* 22, no. 4 (2011): 469–86.

Tully, John. *Devil's Milk: A Social History of Rubber.* New York: Monthly Review Press, 2014.

Whittington, E. Michael, ed. *The Sport of Life and Death: The Mesoamerican Ballgame.* New York: Thames & Hudson, 2001.

Quotation Sources

"These balls jump much more than our hollow balls . . .": Gonzalo Fernández de Oviedo y Valdés, 1535, as quoted in Mann, p. 242.

"Even though lightly thrown . . .": Pietro Martire d'Anghiera, as quoted in Mann, p. 241.

For science teachers everywhere. With thanks.—S. A.

To Michael and Chris, who taught me how to bounce, throw, and shoot
many a sports ball.—E. R. E.

A heartfelt thanks to my expert readers: Dr. Mark Michalovic, Professor of Chemistry,
Bucks County Community College; Mike Tarkanian, Senior Lecturer in the Department of
Materials Science and Engineering at MIT; science teachers James Lehner, Matt Jandreau,
and Amanda Benedict; and to Loree Griffin Burns, scientist and friend.—S. A.

Published by Charlesbridge
9 Galen Street, Watertown, MA 02472
(617) 926-0329
www.charlesbridge.com

Art was created using pen and ink, and watercolor.
Display type set in Fried Cheese © 2003 Bitstream Inc. &
    Font Diner and Chesterfield © 2004 Linotype Library
Text type set in Kennerley © Richard Beatty Designs
Printed by 1010 Printing International Limited in
    Huizhou, Guangdong, China
Production supervision by Jennifer Most Delaney
Designed by Cathleen Schaad

Library of Congress Cataloging-in-Publication Data
Names: Albee, Sarah, author. | Ewen, Eileen Ryan, illustrator.
Title: Bounce!: a scientific history of rubber / Sarah Albee;
    illustrated by Eileen Ryan Ewen.
Description: Watertown, MA: Charlesbridge, [2024] | Includes
    bibliographical references. | Audience: Ages 6–9 | Audience:
    Grades 2–3 | Summary: "Follow the scientific history of
    rubber including who discovered it, where it came from, and
    how it is made. Back matter includes a timeline and a note
    about the social and environmental problems with producing
    rubber."—Provided by publisher.
Identifiers: LCCN 2023029730 (print) | LCCN 2023029731
    (ebook) | ISBN 9781623543792 (hardback) | ISBN
    9781632893574 (ebook)
Subjects: LCSH: Rubber—History—Juvenile literature. |
    Rubber industry and trade—History—Juvenile literature.
    | Science—Juvenile literature. | Inventions—Juvenile
    literature. | Chemistry—Juvenile literature.
Classification: LCC TS1890.A555 2024 (print) | LCC TS1890
    (ebook) | DDC 678/.2 —dc23/eng/20231120
LC record available at https://lccn.loc.gov/2023029730
LC ebook record available at https://lccn.loc.gov/2023029731

Printed in China
(hc) 10 9 8 7 6 5 4 3 2 1